# DESIGNING WITH PATTERN

# *Jan Messent*

# Contents

# Introduction

"Designing with Pattern" has been written specifically to fill a long-felt need for a small concise book about the basic language of pattern.

Originally, the need was my own, having often searched high and low for comforting words of pattern-wisdom and finding only books which were either too general, too specific, too big and expensive, too technical to understand in a hurry, or just plain unattractive. So, I have tried to put into these forty pages the kind of information I needed to know years ago and now have more than a sneaking suspicion that others would find it useful too. However, years later, I find myself in the fortunate but frustrating position of knowing more about pattern than I can comfortably cram into forty pages, which now probably places me among those other pattern-authors whose books were "too-something". Nevertheless, the experience has been such fun, and so theraputic, that I want to share it with you, and this sense of sharing acquired knowledge is what prompted me to handwrite it instead of letting the printer make it look all tidy and impersonal.

The lack of colour has in no way been a disadvantage: quite the contrary, the language of pattern is easier to understand without the added complication of colour to confuse the issue. Not only that, but I would like to feel that the information could be appreciated and used by all craftspeople, whatever their medium, especially those to whom colour is not important.

Those readers who are fairly new to the business of designing patterns will no doubt be interested to know that, like other artistic activities, a strong personal element flows into the process which allows one to hold the guidelines at the back of one's mind while still creating a totally unique piece of work. To me, this is the most satisfying aspect of pattern, that whilst a formula can be taken on board, one is not obliged to be over-awed by it to the point of slavish copying, line by line. So many variables will affect its interpretation, even in the normal course of events, that one might just as well make an extra effort to stretch the guidelines a little further. Once these have been understood and followed for a short distance, one can then let go and play with them, bend them, tie them in knots and eventually break them.

But don't let your enjoyment be dampened by failures. Not every experiment works first time and sometimes days go by without an acceptable result being achieved. Like every other worthwhile activity, practice is essential.

I do hope that using this small book will be an enjoyable experience for you and that, in time, you may come to categorise it as "too useful to do without".

**ABSTRACT**: a design, motif or shape which lacks realism. Geometric designs are abstract, being purely shapes and/or lines, no more. There are various degrees of abstraction, some more meaningful than others.

**CONTRAST**: that part of a design, pattern or shape which is different from its surroundings in terms of colour, tone, texture, shape, size, etc.. The eye regards a contrast as a FOCAL POINT.

**COUNTERCHANGE**: a design or pattern in which the NEGATIVE and POSITIVE shapes change roles to become dominant and subordinate. This is usually achieved by the change over of tones.

**DIAPER**: in textiles, this is synonymous with "all-over-pattern". (SEE SURFACE PATTERN) A pattern in which the borders of one UNIT converge with the borders of its neighbouring REPEAT unit.

**DIRECTION**: describes the way up we are meant to view the pattern. Some patterns have strong lines which lead the eye along them, and this dictates the visual direction. (SEE MULTI-DIRECTIONAL) This pattern has a vertical direction.

**FOCAL POINT**: the part of a design which attracts more attention than the rest. It is often created by some form of contrast, but not all designs or patterns have (or require) a focal point. However, it is a common error to place the focal point in an unsuitable position, thus leading the viewer's attention away from the most important or interesting part instead of enticing the attention towards it. There are many ways of doing this.

**GLOSSARY**

**GRID**: a framework. The structure of lines used to place the pattern-shapes in the correct positions. This may be a network of squares, hexagons, circles, diamonds, etc., and may or may not be left in as part of the pattern.

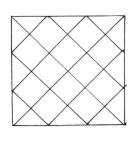

**INTERLACE**: a pattern in which lines pass over and under each other to produce a woven, knotted, chained or laced effect.

**INTERVAL**: the distance between repeated UNITS or MOTIFS. This space can be extended or closed and is just as much a part of the design as the units themselves. (SEE POSITIVE and NEGATIVE)

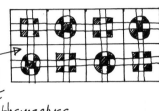

**MEDIUM (plural MEDIA)**: refers to the materials used, e.g. paint, glass, stone, fabric, to translate an idea into a visual form.

**MODIFY**: to refine a design, usually by removing unecessary details and effects which do not transpose successfully into the chosen medium.

**MOTIF or UNIT**: in pattern, this is the repeating element or main shape upon which the design is based. This may not necessarily be an isolated shape; it may be a line or series of lines, but "motif" is a better word than "thing" to describe the main repeat. These are three motifs which have been used on this page.

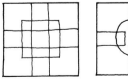 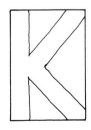

**MULTI-DIRECTIONAL**: a pattern which can be viewed satisfactorily from any direction. (SEE DIRECTION)

**NEGATIVE**: SEE POSITIVE

**PERSPECTIVE** : a system of creating an illusion of three dimensions in objects drawn on a two-dimensional surface.

**POSITIVE and NEGATIVE** : positive shapes (as in photographs) are those which the eye first recognises as being the main motif or unit. This is usually determined by the size, colour, tone and important position of the unit. The spaces between are referred to as negative spaces, but these are just as important to a design and sometimes are made to change roles with the positive ones. (SEE COUNTERCHANGE)

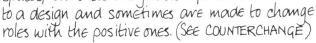

**PROPORTION** : the mathematical relationship of the parts to the whole and to each other. This applies not only to the parts of a pattern, but also to the shape which contains the whole.

**REPEAT** : a pattern which consists of several identical units. It also refers to the method of construction used to place the repeating units.

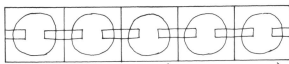

Border repeat pattern   (five repeats used)

**SCALE** : indicates relative or proportionate sizes of UNITS to each other. It also refers to a pattern of overlapping half-circles as on fish. This pattern is also known as scallops and clam-shells.

**SIMPLIFY** (SEE MODIFY) A way of adapting a source of inspiration to make it less complex and more suitable to the designer's needs. It requires a conscious effort in re-designing, using a variety of methods to find the exact stage at which it is suitable for use.

**STENCIL and TEMPLATE** : A shape which has been cut out of (for instance) a piece of paper or wood can be drawn round to make more of the same shapes. This is known

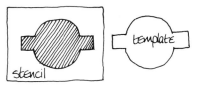

as the template: the "window" is called a stencil.

**SURFACE PATTERN** : units which are repeated in sufficient quantity to cover a surface can be called a surface pattern, even when the units are not all the same size. Man-made patterns are usually built on a GRID which enables the designer to predict the REPEATS accurately.

**SYMBOLIC** : a symbol occurs where the source has been simplified to the greatest possible degree while still retaining its identity.

**SYMMETRY and ASYMMETRY:** a symmetrical motif may be recognised by placing a mirror along a central axis. If the image in the mirror and the reflected half together reproduce the complete design — EXACTLY — then the motif is symmetrical. If there are differences, the motif is said to be asymmetrical, though it may still be perfectly balanced.

**STYLISE (or STYLIZE):** to modify or otherwise transpose the essential properties of an idea to make it suitable for a designer's chosen medium. To SIMPLIFY and MODIFY are part of this process. Beware of adopting stylized interpretations meant for other media just because they have been simplified. This does not necessarily make them suitable for the technique you have chosen to use: the requirements of your technique must be acknowledged and understood.

**TECHNIQUE** : the practical/mechanical means used together with the MEDIUM, by which the designer translates a design. "Good technique" is used to refer to the standard of this mechanical process, and implies that the designer has understood its uses and knows how to exploit them. It does not necessarily refer to the design, though ideally both should be of the same high standard. It is when this aim is achieved that the designer may feel that at last he has reached some degree of proficiency.

**UNIT** : SEE MOTIF

**Informal Pattern.** Freestyle patterns can often be drawn, without the use of grids or other constructional aids, to cover limited areas. A pattern can also be drawn freehand if it is to be repeated only approximately, not exactly, in which case any differences in the repeats will actually be desirable. Above are some simple patterns where the repeating elements are only similar, not exact. The differences make them more interesting than if the spaces and shapes were all of the same size. Patterns like this can be found in nature, e.g. shells, scales, hair, pebbles, bubbles, water, etc.. They are extremely useful to designers for creating areas of informal texture and background pattern. Collect ideas in drawings, photos and cuttings for your notebook.

**Pattern and Rhythm.** Rhythm is inbuilt into patterns merely by repetition, but some patterns are better examples of this phenomenon than others. It is best typified by a feeling of controlled movement, a flow of lines and/or shapes rather than an overall covering of repeated elements. To have rhythm, a pattern requires some means by which the eye can be carried along into the repeating elements, backwards and forwards, up and down, easily and with purpose. As the eye finds it easier to travel along <u>lines</u> rather than to hop from one unit to another, those patterns which have lines in them will usually also contain the strongest rhythms, but if <u>shapes</u> are placed so closely together that they form a line, they will have the same effect. See below for examples of rhythm.

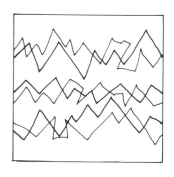
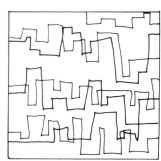

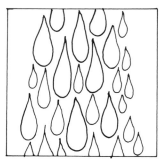

**Pattern Provokes a Response.** Apart from being merely a decoration on a surface, pattern has another, and arguably, more meaningful role of conveying to the viewer a message (however simple) and of provoking a response. It would be a pity to ignore this element in the process of designing as, to the viewer (and maybe to a potential buyer!), this may be a very important deciding factor in the acceptance or rejection, understanding or misunderstanding of the object upon which the pattern is placed.

Leaving aside, for the moment, considerations such as colour and scale, both of them response-provoking in a different way, the _form_ of the pattern must be appropriate. Pictorial elements are easy to interpret; abstract ones dig deeper down into the subconscious and the designer should make some attempt to question and find answers to this phenomenon.
The illustrations here give some indication of the possibilities.

a. Shattered, broken, fragmented, upset, angry. Lightning, breakages, frost.
b. Undulating, peaceful, gentle movement, rocking. Clouds, water, fields, bed/blankets.
c. Movement v. stasis. Conflict, opposition. Buildings, shelter against the elements.
d. Barrier; stop. Tension. Expectancy. Netting, a fence.
e. Growth, upsurge, action, new life. Plant forms, springtime.
f. Pressure downwards from above; conversely, pushing upwards. Underground supports.
g. Whoosh! Swift upward movement, or downwards.
h. Haven, safety, a way in and a way out. Pod shape, womb, pocket or purse.

Below: tracing of a street plan (Susan Messent)

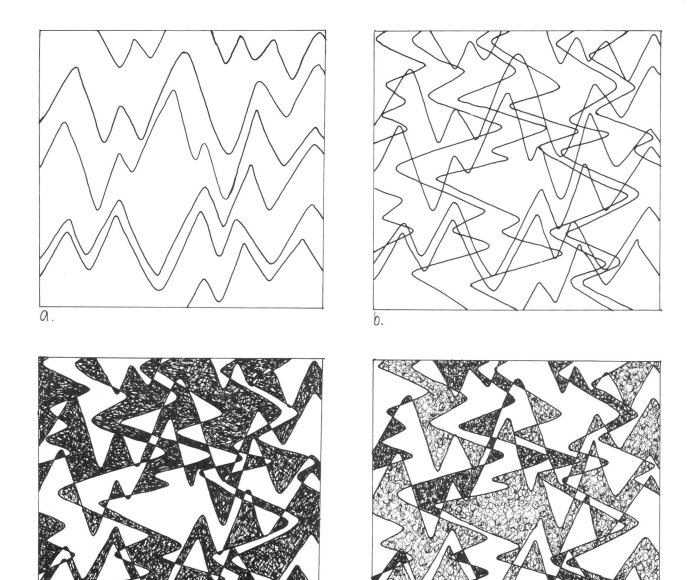

a.

b.

c.

d.

Informal patterns may be translated into any technique just as they are, sometimes with little or no adaptation. However, to be more original and interesting, one can develop an informal pattern in a variety of ways. One of these is to overlay a tracing on top of another one in a different direction, or upside down. As soon as one set of lines crosses another, shapes are formed, allowing for the use of tonal changes, colour and texture. This is what has happened here.

a.   An informal pattern of zig-zag lines flows from one side of a square to the other.
      Try this experiment on any reasonably simple pattern. Use any shape "container".
b.   A tracing of a. is now placed over the top so that the new lines flow vertically, forming
      shapes where they cross. It is good that some of these are larger than others.
c.   Two-tone shading has now established a "positive/negative" effect. The relative sizes of the
      shapes now becomes more obvious and will no doubt suggest the next development stage.
d.   This is the same as c. but now positive becomes negative and an extra tone has been added.

e.

f.

Another method, used alone or in conjunction with overlaying, is to cut a pattern into sections. Always leave the original intact when you use this method: take several tracings or photo-copies on which to experiment.

e. This is a. shaded in 4 tones, cut into 16 and re-arranged to form another square.

f. Again, a. shaded in 4 tones, cut into 8 oblongs and re-arranged to flow in both directions.

g. Basically same as f. but now centre square from c. added. This changes the scale and also adds another, sharper, tone.

h. 4 vertical strips cut from b. and 4 from d.. Unequal widths, placed out of sequence. Some dividing lines removed. This development combines both tracing and cutting, as does g.

g.

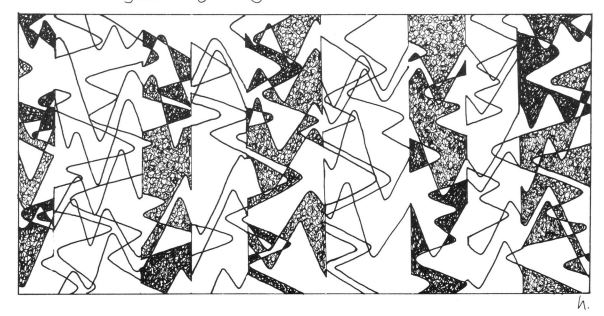

h.

One of the simplest forms of pattern-making
is the old childhood activity of folded cut paper.
This is especially successful on paper which
is already patterned, remembering that
the reverse sides present a paler
range of tones. Where two of the
same tones "collide", the edges
disappear to create a
soft, shadowy effect.

Pattern
superimposed
on pattern.

## Cut Paper Patterns

A page of cut paper experiments, even in tones of black and white, creates a richness of shapes and textures. Make use of the following ideas:
patterned paper and carrier bags
handmade and painted papers
wrapping (especially marbled) papers
wallpaper offcuts and borders
drawer lining paper, white + metallic d'oylies
coloured tissue papers
coloured gummed squares, shapes, etc.
magazine pages and greetings cards

Try the following methods:
1. Wide strips, folded and cut into borders.
2. Circles and squares, folded and cut.
3. Narrow strips woven together.
4. Small squares re-arranged to make an abstract patchwork.
5. Superimpose any of these methods over the top of each other or over more patterned paper. This breaks up the pattern of both pieces.

Pencil drawing of a piece of malachite, from a photograph in a book, using a very limited number of tones as part of the simplification process. The drawing is then photocopied several times.
One of these is cut into measured squares and 12 of these are re-arranged, at random. The blank spaces are carefully positioned to balance the arrangement and the direction of each square is planned to direct the eye into the centre, across the gaps and on to the next one.

We are now moving one step nearer to organised pattern: as our experiments become more complex we find that we need the help of a framework (i.e. a grid) which will help us to construct and balance the various elements of our patterns.

The scale, and the area covered by the grid are entirely the choice of the designer.

## Organisation in Pattern

We are always impressed by order and rhythm in nature. Though many patterns appear to be complex and haphazard, in fact this is not so, as there are mathematical formulae for every one of nature's patterns.

Man finds order preferable, and easier to understand, than disorder. Apart from this natural preference, when a unit must be repeated precisely over a large area, sometimes by machine, a means must be found to do this easily and quickly.

So each unit is placed on a grid which helps to organise the placement of each pattern repeat.

order, regiment

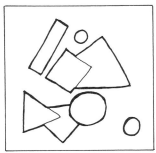

disorder, scatter

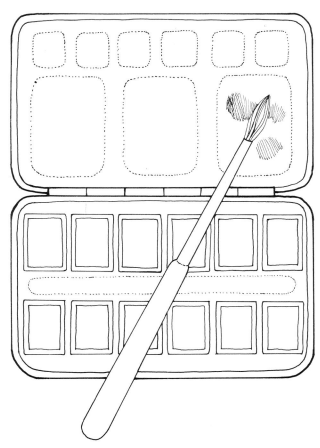

Make a reference file of nature's and man's examples of organised pattern —

Snowflakes and microscopic organisms, shells (inside and cross-sections), leaves, water, honeycomb, etc..

Things in boxes (chocolates, paints), wiring systems, scaffolding, machinery, etc..

The grids shown on the next page are as follows:

a. and b: six-sided figures on isometric paper.
c. Hexagon, shaded to look like a cube.
d. Square diamonds on a square grid.
e. Long diamonds.
f. Interlocking triangles.
g. Triangles on a square grid.
h. Other triangles made from squares.
i. and o. Octogons, when joined together, leave small squares between.
j. Square grid.
k. l. p and q. Half-drop grids
m. Diamond grid.
n. Scale, scallop or clam-shell grid.
r. Square diamonds divided into triangles.
s. Long diamond grid, also forming triangles.

GRIDS : These are some of the simplest grids used
as frameworks upon which some patterns are based.
The grid-lines may either be removed when planning is
complete, or left in to become part of the pattern.
Whilst a grid can be used as a framework for placing
motifs at regular and precise intervals, the grid alone
constitutes a pattern without anything inside the
shapes. Fabric patchwork is produced on the basis of
plain or patterned shapes which inter-relate on a grid
system.
On this basis, we can say that a pattern depends
sometimes on the repetition of a single motif, either
formally or at random, sometimes on the repetition of
a variety of motifs in a particular formation, and
sometimes on a grid construction alone.

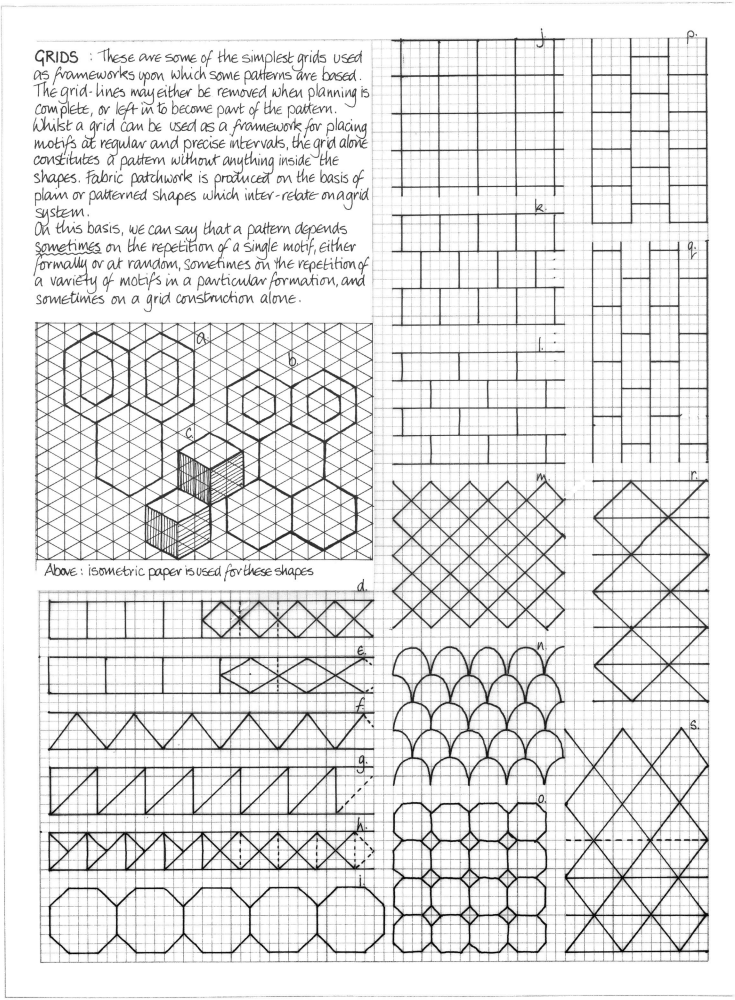

Above: isometric paper is used for these shapes

## Using a Grid

In simple terms, the illustrations show how a grid is used to plan a structured pattern, though there are unlimited variations possible, some of which will be dealt with further on.

There is no rule about which comes first, the motif or the grid; this will depend on the technique you are using, personal requirements, and so on. Neither is there a rule about what shape of grid to use with a particular type of motif; this will be discovered at the designing stage.

Example 1.

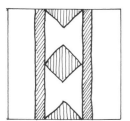 

A square unit containing the design to be repeated.

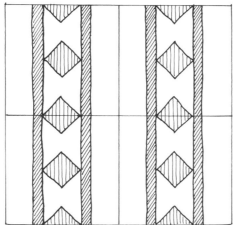

4 units fit together and the pattern begins to emerge.

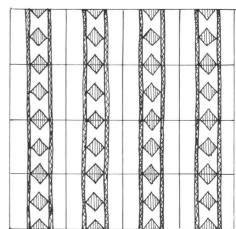

16 units show a definite stripe. This is a vertical pattern.

Example 2.

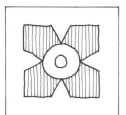

A spot motif does not link like no. 1.

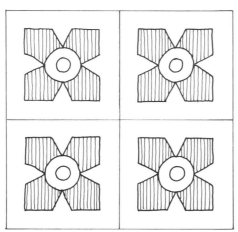

4 units fit together to form a spot pattern.

The grid lines may be removed once the pattern begins to take shape.

Example 3.

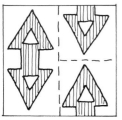

A square unit divided into a half-drop shows how a motif drops half-way down at one side.

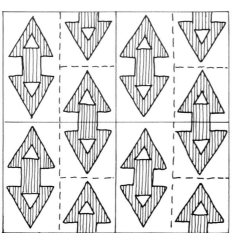

This is how they link over 4 repeats.

16 units (repeats) show how the motifs interlock as a result of the half-drop arrangement.

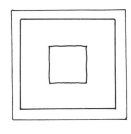

Simple squares set inside each other can be divided further by diagonal lines.

  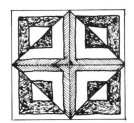

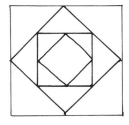

Squares set diagonally create triangles and diamonds.

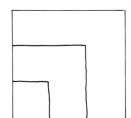

Two overlapping squares from opposite corners create three small squares.

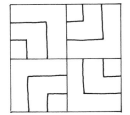 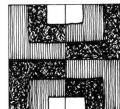 

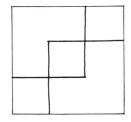

Three overlapping squares create two L-shapes.

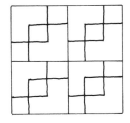 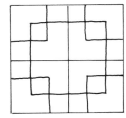 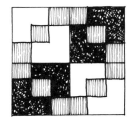

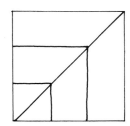

This is the same unit as above with an added diagonal creating even more possibilities.

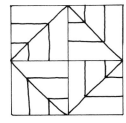 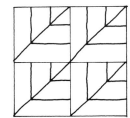 

More simple square units to use in multiple combinations of four, sixteen or more.

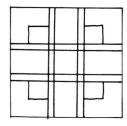 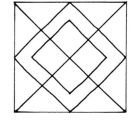 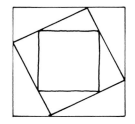 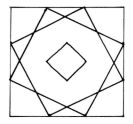

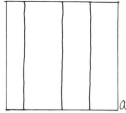 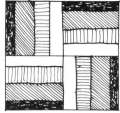 a.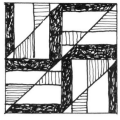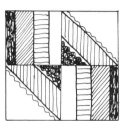

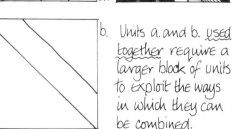
b. Units a. and b. used together require a larger block of units to exploit the ways in which they can be combined.

Blocks of 16 units using 8 of a. and 8 of b.

Use a pad of squared paper (5 squares to the inch) to work out patterns of squares, strips and diagonals. An extra diagonal line across a unit of straight lines can create dozens more arrangements of 2, 3 or more tones. Even without colour, textures can be substituted, and the use of counterpoint can, in effect, double the potential of the original unit. Look in books on patchwork for other ideas on square grid patterns, but avoid copying these slavishly; try your own.

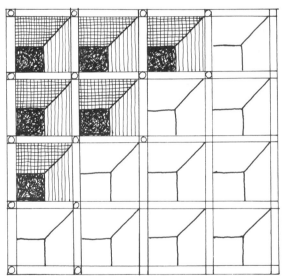

Left: this simple square unit, shaded in three tones, gives an impression of three dimensions. Below: these two patterns remind one of the complex textile designs of Ancient Peru but are quite simply the product of the single unit in the centre. When shaded negative/positive the eye becomes confused, even more so when the unit is turned at an angle. Many more arrangements are possible, made easier by making several tracings, cutting them out and fitting them together again in different positions.

"A Page from the Book of Kells" (the author) A canvas embroidered frame encloses the figure of St. John, from the Book of Kells, using the same squared border pattern as that seen on the edge of the page. See the drawing below. The colours were carefully blended to imitate the faded rose-pinks, blues, burnished gold and parchment tones of the manuscript.

Below left: a patchwork experiment using crochet squares of random-dyed yarns and patterned paper. This is one method of designing in squares which helps one to discover how multi-coloured yarns behave over small areas. It also allows one to work out the balance of colour and texture in the pattern before starting the full-scale project.

Below right: woven strips of paper, a wrapped card frame and a small sample of knitting are used on this squared colour experiment.

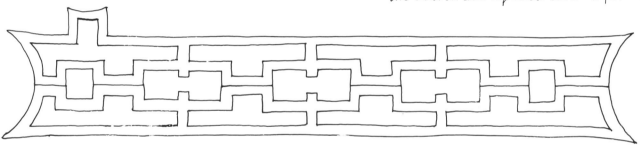

"Tulip Mirror" by Barbara Dunhill

This delightful embroidered mirror-frame gives the appearance of square ceramic tiles often seen in old Dutch interiors. Although no square is exactly the same as another, the repetition and overall balance makes a strong pattern which leads the eye around the central mirror space. The eye is then halted by a little grub on one of the bulbs and this then leads to a closer search for more of the same. There are no less than eight different creatures to be seen, two butterflies, two wasps, two snails, one slug and a caterpillar. A neat change of scale is achieved by the addition of a fine zig-zag border all round which has the effect of holding the eye in.

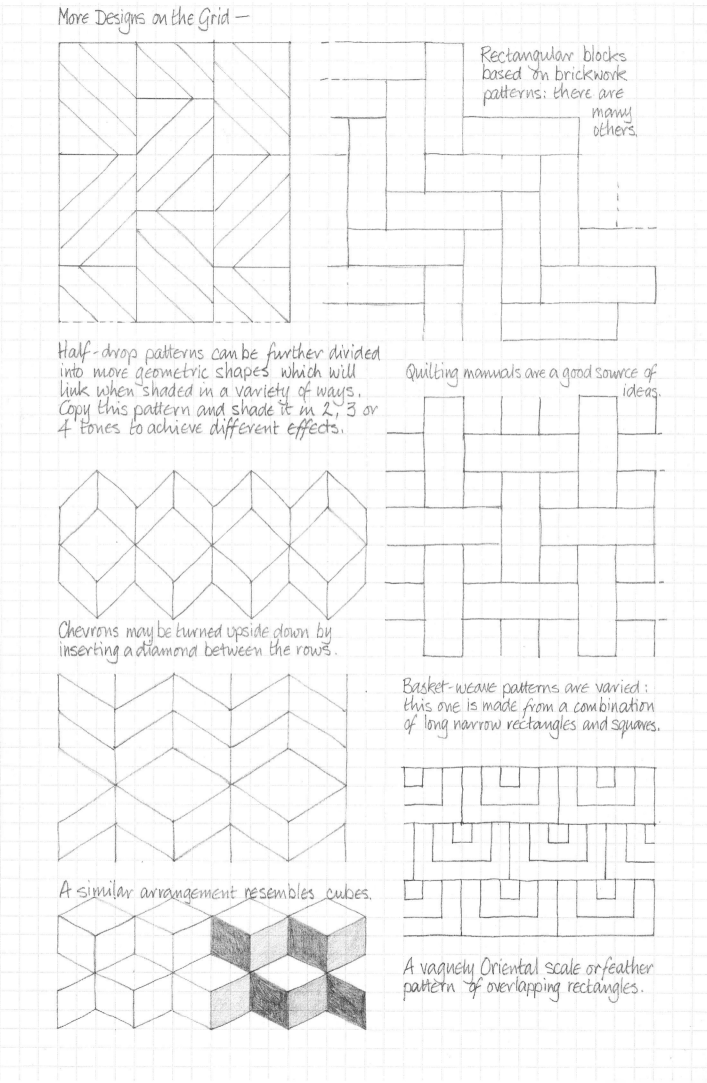

Rectangular blocks based on brickwork patterns: there are many others.

Half-drop patterns can be further divided into more geometric shapes which will link when shaded in a variety of ways. Copy this pattern and shade it in 2, 3 or 4 tones to achieve different effects.

Quilting manuals are a good source of ideas.

Chevrons may be turned upside down by inserting a diamond between the rows.

Basket-weave patterns are varied; this one is made from a combination of long narrow rectangles and squares.

A similar arrangement resembles cubes.

A vaguely Oriental scale or feather pattern of overlapping rectangles.

This repeat of half-circles is known as the scale, scallop, clam-shell or feather pattern.
Decoration inside each shape can be very varied and may follow the outline of the top curve, or
accentuate the radiating lines springing from each point.
Construction: draw parallel lines at equal distances apart on which to base the half-circles,
then use a compass to draw half-circles which just touch each other as well as the line above
them. Make the shapes of each row fit exactly half-way between those on the row above.
Rub out the construction lines.

## The Circle as a Grid

Within circles, the most commonly used pattern arrangements tend to fall under the following headings:

Radiating lines with points to the centre (as on a bicycle wheel).
Radiating lines with points to the circumference (as for a star).
Concentric circles (as with ripples).
Divided across the centre to make a symmetrical pattern in two halves —
        or top to tail.
Spirals (as on a watch-spring).
Moving circles (as with a water-wheel and its angled projections).
Any combination of the above.


Below: *four developments/variations on a theme.*
Many more changes to the basic pattern can be made, all of which will appear different when the shading is varied. This is a rewarding exercise which helps to develop inventiveness in pattern-making and an eye for balance between the negative and positive shapes.

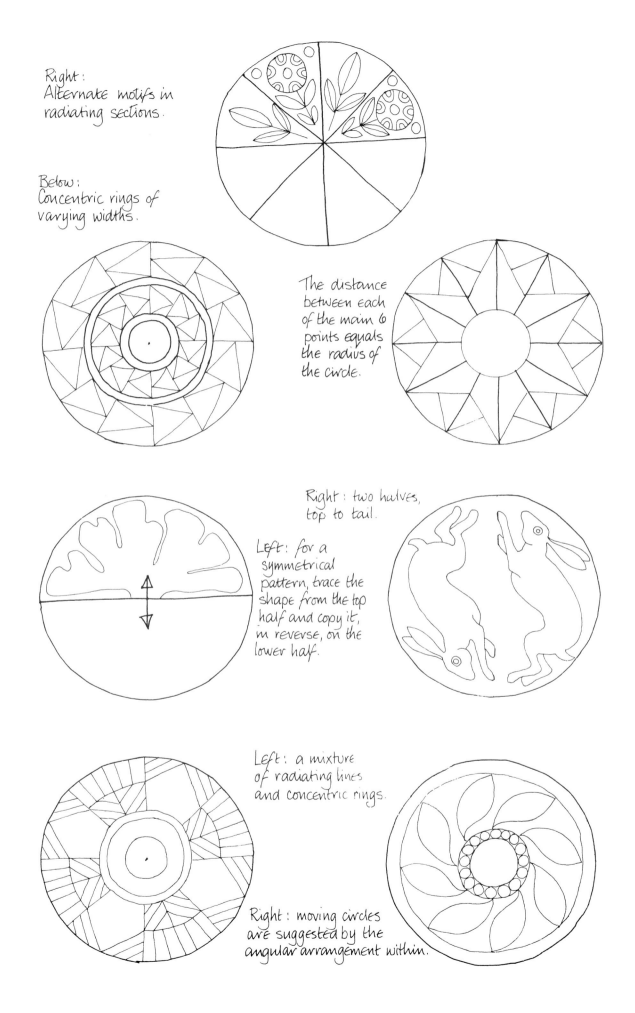

Right:
Alternate motifs in radiating sections.

Below:
Concentric rings of varying widths.

The distance between each of the main 6 points equals the radius of the circle.

Right: two halves, top to tail.

Left: for a symmetrical pattern, trace the shape from the top half and copy it, in reverse, on the lower half.

Left: a mixture of radiating lines and concentric rings.

Right: moving circles are suggested by the angular arrangement within.

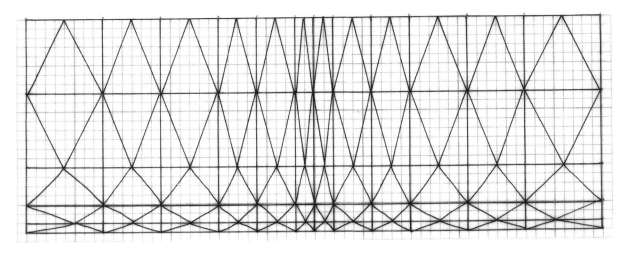

The vertical lines are widest apart on the side edges of this panel : they close up towards the centre. The horizontal lines are widest apart at the top, closing up towards the bottom. All diagonal lines are constructed from two corners of each rectangle towards the centre of the next line — except in two cases !

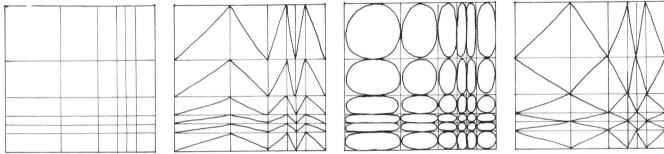

Shapes inside these distorted grids create a feeling of compression and curves.
Below: curves created on a square grid, with straight lines, leap across one, two or three squares.

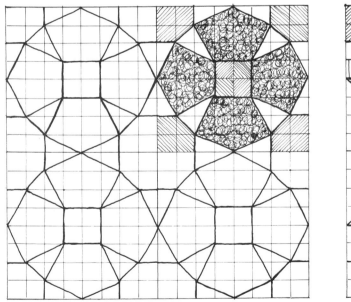

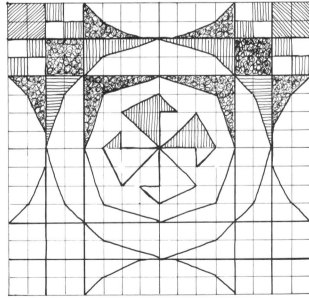

Each of the above designs is based on one unit repeated four times. Note the line-spacing in the example below.

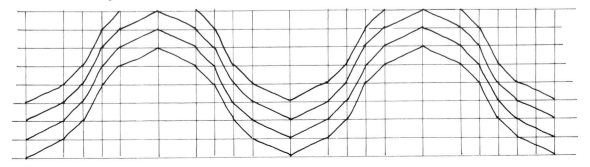

# Distorting the Grid

On the opposite page, formal grid lines are spaced at various intervals though their regularity still creates a predictable pattern. However, free-style distortion of grid-lines is less predictable, as well as being great fun to do. Use straight and curved lines in any combination, or draw a simple motif superimposed onto a distorted grid.

Suggestions, seen below, include:

1. Straight lines in both directions.
2. Curved lines, emphasising the shapes. } All these are open to other interpretations.
3. Straight and curved lines together.
4. Curved lines over a regular grid.

The spaces/shapes produced by any of these methods can be shaded in 2 or more tones, or textured, (see the Informal Pattern page), or coloured, or filled with other random patterns. The results may be used as the basis of a single design on a large scale, or to plan an all-over pattern using the blocks in a grid system, thus creating grids within a larger one. To avoid over-complication, it may be necessary to include some blank (empty) blocks here and there.

1.

2.

3.

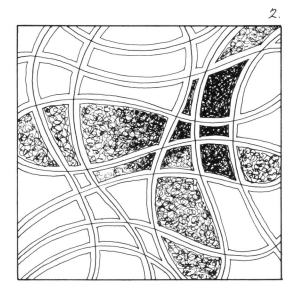

4.

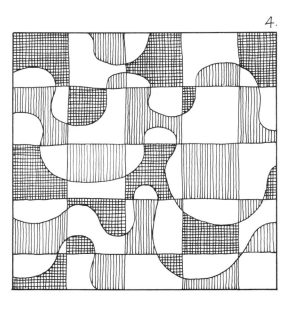

# Designing the Motif (1.)

More or less any shapes, even familiar household objects, can be converted into decorative motifs. Simple shapes are best to begin with; a letter from the alphabet, a number, a leaf, a flower-head.

Symmetrical motifs are easy to draw, but asymmetrical ones usually produce more unpredictable, and therefore more interesting patterns.

Do not assume that there is only one best shape to contain your chosen motif. A rounded flower-head will also fit into a triangle, a hexagon, a diamond and a square, just as a straight-sided shape will fit into a circle or 'scallop'.

These examples show how a simple motif (the letter K) has been tried out in various shapes to discover what negative spaces are produced.
REMEMBER: the negative areas are part of the pattern too and must be as interesting as the motif itself.

The first sketch may not be the most successful — it rarely is, even for experienced designers! It may take quite a lot of "doodling" before a satisfactory arrangement appears, but this is quite normal.

The next stage is to discover what effects will be produced when these newly-formed units are joined together. There are many ways of doing this. The unit may be arranged to form a block, (as in a. opposite page), or it may be repeated to form its own grid pattern, (as in b.).
A block may be repeated on a grid, or as a border, or used as an isolated unit for a decorative panel.

To try out these new arrangements, trace the original unit onto good quality tracing paper. This allows one to make use of both the right and reverse sides (as in d.) and duplication will be more accurate than drawing round a small template. Re-trace the unit in different positions, and from both sides, to form blocks and all-over patterns.

See the following pages for more suggestions.

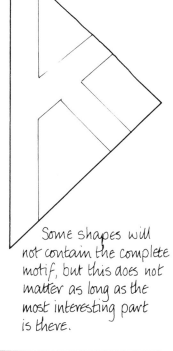

Some shapes will not contain the complete motif, but this does not matter as long as the most interesting part is there.

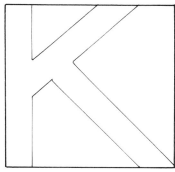

Taking parts of the motif into corners and to half-way points along the sides makes it more probable that they will link with each other —

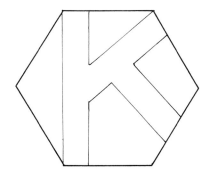

when joined together. The motif may have to be re-drawn to make this happen if it helps to produce a more interesting pattern.

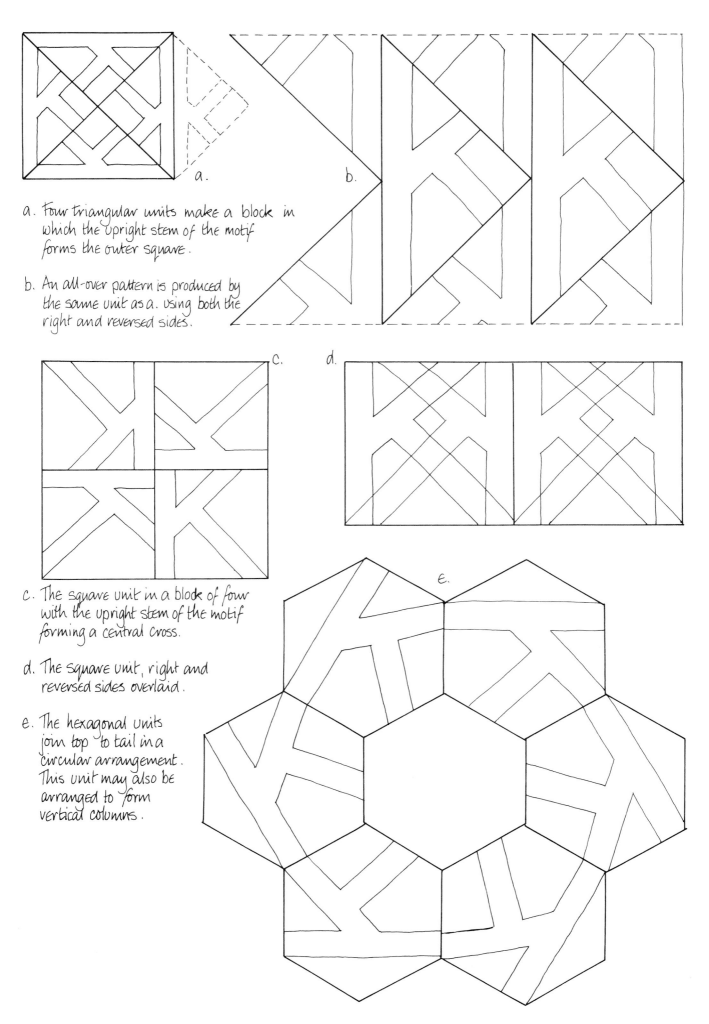

a. Four triangular units make a block in which the upright stem of the motif forms the outer square.

b. An all-over pattern is produced by the same unit as a. using both the right and reversed sides.

c. The square unit in a block of four with the upright stem of the motif forming a central cross.

d. The square unit, right and reversed sides overlaid.

e. The hexagonal units join top to tail in a circular arrangement. This unit may also be arranged to form vertical columns.

## Designing the Motif (2)

Think of a number......... and then forget its significance and think of it instead as merely an interesting shape.

1. Draw a large number onto soft card, several inches high, and refine it until you have an attractive shape. Then cut it out and use it as a template.

2. On a large piece of plain paper, draw round the number —
   a. at different angles
   b. upside down and sideways
   c. reversed
   d. linking and interlocking
   e. inside different grid shapes
   f. trace it and cut the tracing across; then re-trace it in different positions and overlap them.
   g. make borders......... the list is endless......

## Border Patterns

The motif for this border pattern was derived from a photograph of white chairs and tables on a

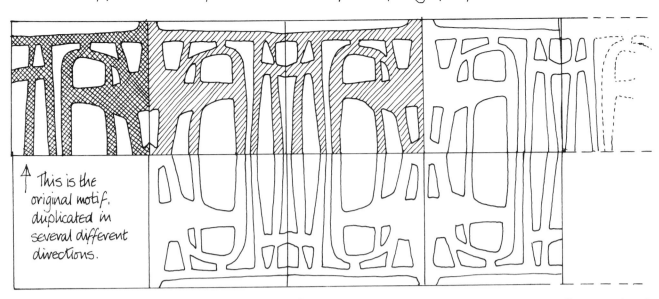

↑ This is the original motif, duplicated in several different directions.

terrace. A tracing was taken to simplify the shapes and to exclude unecessary details, and also to accentuate the negative shapes between the pieces of furniture. A small "window" was cut out of white paper to enclose an interesting section of the tracing and this was then transferred to more tracing-paper laid over the window. This motif is then traced several more times, these are cut into separate pieces and re-arranged in a variety of ways. This pattern (above) shows mirror-images of the original, and this has been duplicated underneath with another set of mirror-images to produce an interesting arrangement of large and smaller shapes.

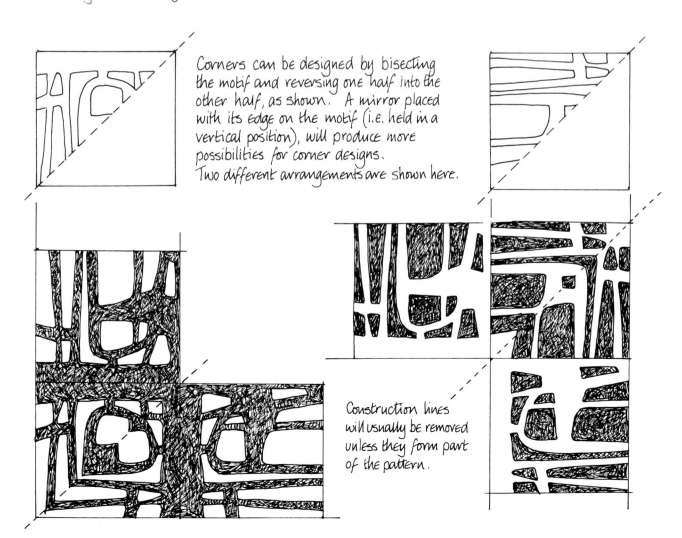

Corners can be designed by bisecting the motif and reversing one half into the other half, as shown. A mirror placed with its edge on the motif (i.e. held in a vertical position), will produce more possibilities for corner designs.
Two different arrangements are shown here.

Construction lines will usually be removed unless they form part of the pattern.

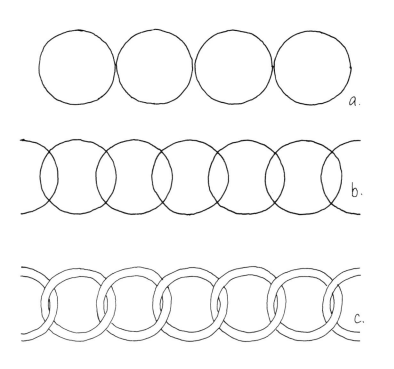

a.

b.

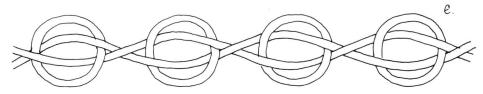

c.

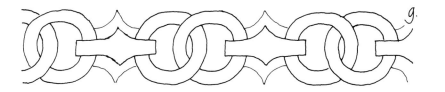

d.

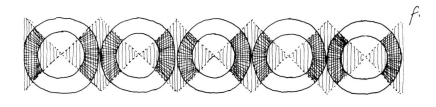

e.

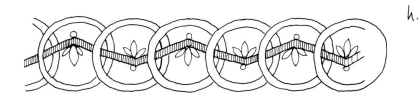

These diagrams illustrate how a simple motif, in this case a circle, can be positioned to form a variety of border patterns. The same methods can be applied to other more complex motifs:

a. motifs may be linked by just touching,

b. overlapping in any proportion,

c. linking into each other,

d. by using some form of linking device,

e. by using a line to connect them,

f. by placing another secondary motif in the background or alongside,

or by any combination of these methods.

g. Links, with a connecting device.

h. Overlaps with a continuous line.

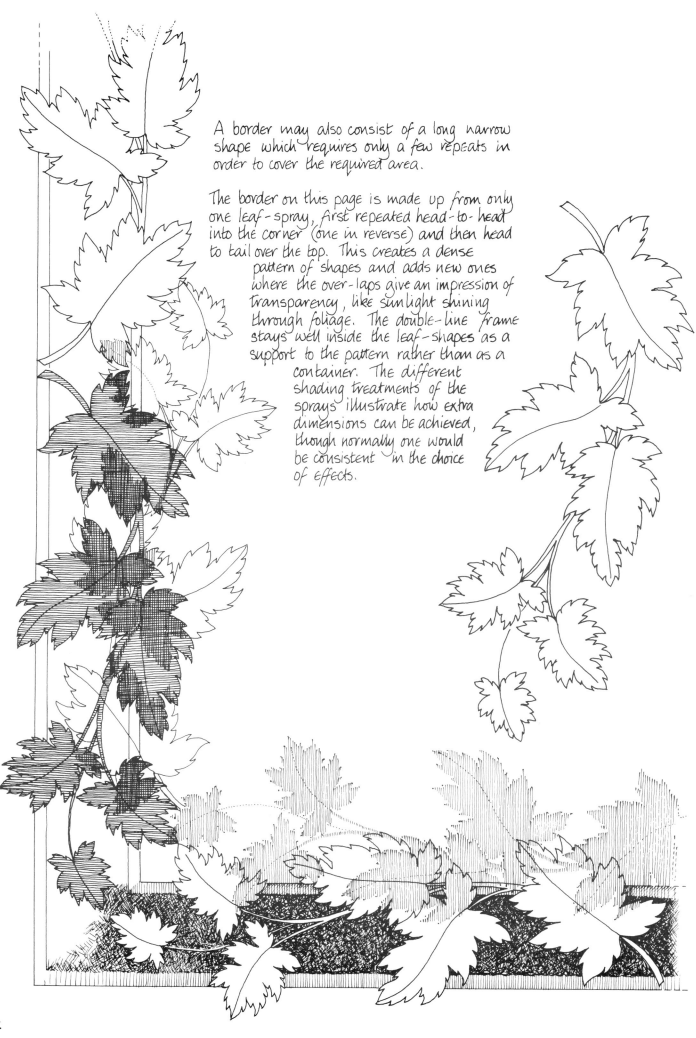

A border may also consist of a long narrow shape which requires only a few repeats in order to cover the required area.

The border on this page is made up from only one leaf-spray, first repeated head-to-head into the corner (one in reverse) and then head to tail over the top. This creates a dense pattern of shapes and adds new ones where the over-laps give an impression of transparency, like sunlight shining through foliage. The double-line frame stays well inside the leaf-shapes as a support to the pattern rather than as a container. The different shading treatments of the sprays illustrate how extra dimensions can be achieved, though normally one would be consistent in the choice of effects.

The treatment of the background spaces should be designed with the chosen technique in mind. The top of the border may not require a straight edge: the background may be further patterned or textured and the motif left void, or vice-versa.

In a "one-way-up" pattern like this one, a different motif may have to be devised for the corners, especially if it is to be a different shape also. This must, of course, bear a close relationship to the main motif. Use tracing-paper to try out several ideas before deciding, and allow the background treatment to help with the unity and the continuity of the pattern.

## Borders as All-over Patterns

Below :
This collage jumper design is made from strips of newspaper and white paper d'oylie.
Seen from a distance, it has the appearance of an abstract pattern which is balanced,
though not symmetrical.   Border patterns can be used collectively in this way either
vertically, like this one, or horizontally, or even diagonally, to create all-over patterns.
Plain spaces of different widths between the patterned rows help to define and give
"breathing space" to the busier parts, but this is a matter of personal choice and is not a rule.

Opposite page : a pattern project —
Use squared paper (5 squares to the inch) to plan blocks of pattern with simple shapes,
allowing them to merge with each other and to overlap.  It is interesting to discover that a
study of this kind can actually generate ideas as the pattern develops ; shapes form
out of lines that cross and negative spaces suddenly become the basis of the next block.
    Cut up bits of old photographs, postcards and patterned paper to add more
complicated shapes, and extend lines from the edges of these into the next area.
    This "doodle" page, even without colour, is an excellent way of learning to adjust
busy and plain areas,  how to balance shapes of different sizes  and how to understand
the significance of every detail in the overall scheme.

## See-Through Patterns

Patterns are often imposed on objects and views in the form of window-panes, fences or gateways. Photographs reveal a wealth of ideas which can be used as a grid (as in patchwork) or can become an element in an informal pattern, like those on the opposite page.

Other see-through patterns include netting (fruit, vegetables, fish, curtains): wire-netting (hens, rabbits, scenery): wrought iron (country & town houses, balconies, railway stations): trellis (flowers and creepers): basket-work (lobster pots, pets).

Patterns <u>behind</u> things include table cloths, carpets and rugs, patterned plates, reflections, wood-grained surfaces, etc..

The design elements here are —
   the window frame
   the trees
   the background.
The way we choose to treat these elements will have the effect of making one (or parts of one) more dominant than the others.

The simplicity or complexity of the results must depend partly on your chosen technique and medium, and partly on your own personal preference.

All of these examples are perfectly acceptable as balanced informal patterns.

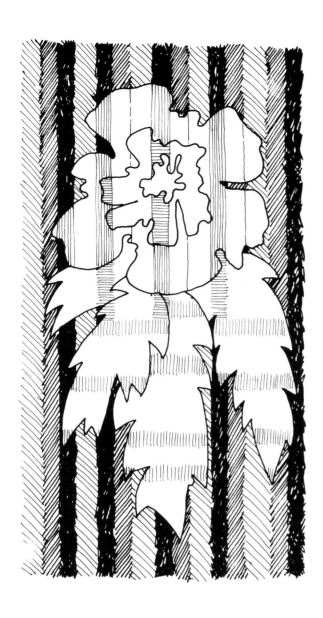

Lay a tracing — of a flower, for instance, — over lined or chequered paper (you can make this yourself on graph paper) and shade in some of the stripes, either inside the shape or on the background. Try this also on other patterns found on wrapping paper or in magazines and scrapbooks.

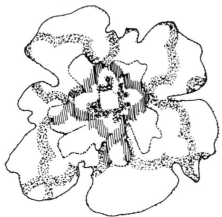

# How to Construct Polygons

You will need a compass, a protractor (for measuring angles), a ruler and a pencil. If you draw these shapes on thin card, they can be cut out and used as templates for drawing round.

## Pentagon

1. Using a compass, draw a circle of the size you want the pentagon to be.

2. Mark the centre and a point anywhere on the circumference.

3. Line up these 2 points as shown on the right.

4. Mark the 72° point. If this is well outside the edge of the circle, because the protractor is larger, no matter. Mark it off just the same.

5. Now move the protractor round, keeping the centre point over the centre of the circle, and mark off 3 more 72° points as before, each time placing the 0° on the last mark on the circumference of the circle.

6. This will produce 5 points, equally spaced, either on the circle or just beyond it.
   If the points are beyond the circumference, take a ruler and line this up from point to centre. Now mark the circle where the ruler crosses it.

7. Join up all 5 points to produce a PENTAGON.

## Hexagon

Proceed as for a pentagon, but marking off 60° points all round the circle. Then join up the six points.
   The other way of doing this, without a protractor, is to keep the compass at the same radius as that used to draw the circle. Place the compass point on the circumference of the circle and mark off the radius where the pencil point bisects the circle. Remove the point of the compass, replace it on one of the marks and continue to mark off the same measurement all round the circle until there are 6 equally-spaced marks. Now join these together using a ruler.

## Octogon

Proceed as for a pentagon but marking off 45° points all round the circle. Then join up the 8 points. An octogon can also be constructed quite easily on graph paper.

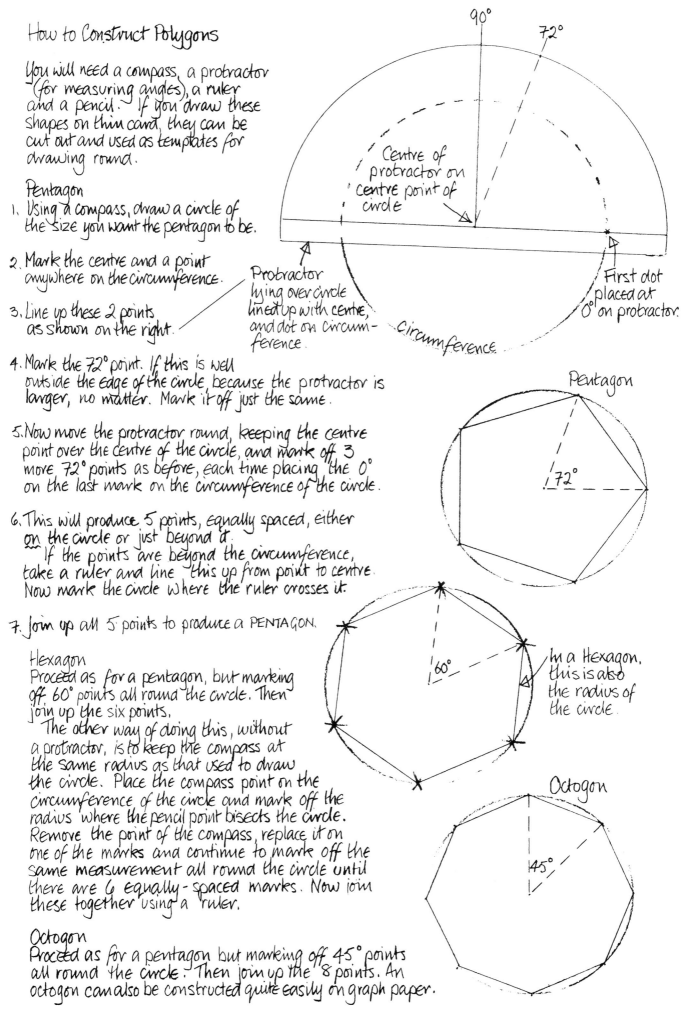

90°    72°

Centre of protractor on centre point of circle

Protractor lying over circle lined up with centre, and dot on circumference.

Circumference

First dot placed at 0° on protractor.

Pentagon

72°

60°

In a Hexagon, this is also the radius of the circle.

Octogon

45°

# Manipulated Patterns

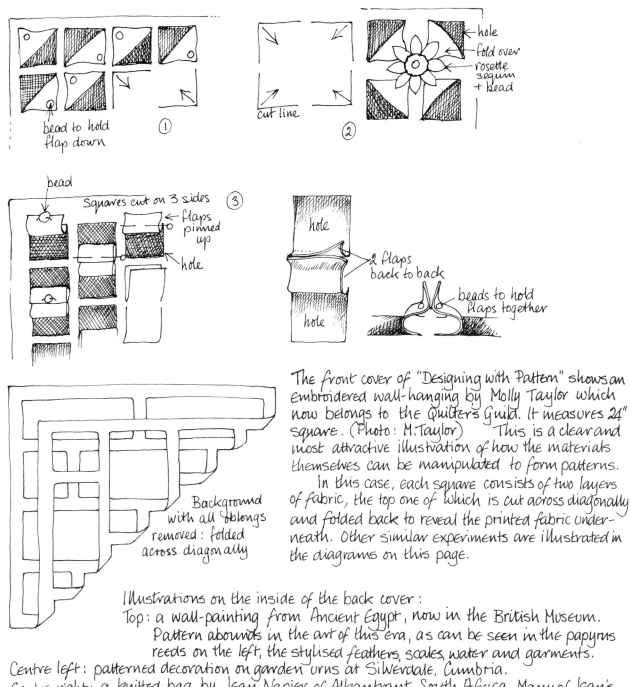

The front cover of "Designing with Pattern" shows an embroidered wall-hanging by Molly Taylor which now belongs to the Quilters Guild. It measures 24" square. (Photo: M. Taylor)  This is a clear and most attractive illustration of how the materials themselves can be manipulated to form patterns.

In this case, each square consists of two layers of fabric, the top one of which is cut across diagonally and folded back to reveal the printed fabric underneath. Other similar experiments are illustrated in the diagrams on this page.

Illustrations on the inside of the back cover:

Top: a wall-painting from Ancient Egypt, now in the British Museum. Pattern abounds in the art of this era, as can be seen in the papyrus reeds on the left, the stylised feathers, scales, water and garments.

Centre left: patterned decoration on garden urns at Silverdale, Cumbria.

Centre right: a knitted bag by Jean Napier of Alkantrant, South Africa. Many of Jean's bags are inspired by the Viennese artist Friedrich Hundertwasser.

Below: a corner of the large topiary garden at Levens Hall in Cumbria, probably the most innovative and exciting of its kind in the U.K.

Back cover: coloured pencil patterns.

Except for Molly Taylor's wall-hanging, Barbara Dunhill's Tulip Mirror and Jean Napier's knitted bag, all other photographs and artworks are by the author, who wishes to thank these three friends for their generosity in so willingly allowing her to use their work in this book.